Novels for Students, Volume 1

Since this page cannot legibly accommodate all copyright notices, the acknowledgments constitute an extension of the copyright notice.

While every effort has been made to secure permission to reprint material and to ensure the reliability of the information presented in this publication, Gale Research neither guarantees the accuracy of the data contained herein nor assumes any responsibility for errors, omissions or discrepancies. Gale accepts no payment for listing; and inclusion in the publication of any organization, agency, institution, publication, service, or individual does not imply endorsement of the editors or publisher. Errors brought to the attention of the publisher and verified to the satisfaction of the publisher will be corrected in future editions.

This publication is a creative work fully protected by all applicable copyright laws, as well as by misappropriation, trade secret, unfair competition, and other applicable laws. The authors and editors of this work have added value to the underlying factual material herein through one or more of the following: unique and original selection, coordination, expression, arrangement, and classification of the information.

All rights to this publication will be vigorously defended.

Copyright © 1997
Gale Research
835 Penobscot Building
645 Griswold St.
Detroit, Ml 48226-4094

All rights reserved including the right of reproduction in whole or in part in any form.

This book is printed on acid-free paper that meets the minimum requirements of American National Standard for Information Sciences—Permanence Paper for Printed Library Materials, ANSI Z39.48-1984.

ISBN 0-7876-1686-9
ISSN 1094-3552

Printed in the United States of America
10 9 8 7 6 5

The Adventures of Huckleberry Finn

Mark Twain 1884

Introduction

Although probably no other work of American literature has been the source of so much controversy, Mark Twain's *The Adventures of Huckleberry Finn* is regarded by many as the greatest literary achievement America has yet produced. Inspired by many of the author's own experiences as a river-boat pilot, the book tells of two runaways—a white boy and a black man—and their journey down the mighty Mississippi River. When the book first appeared, it scandalized reviewers and parents who thought it would corrupt young children with its depiction of a hero who lies, steals, and uses coarse language. In the last half of the twentieth century, the condemnation of the book has continued on the grounds that its portrayal of Jim and use of the word "nigger' is racist. The novel continues to appear on lists of books banned in schools across the country.

Nevertheless, from the beginning *The Adventures of Huckleberry Finn* was also recognized as a book that would revolutionize American literature. The strong point of view, skillful depiction of dialects, and confrontation of issues of race and prejudice have inspired critics to dub it *"the* great American novel." Nobel Prize-winning author Ernest Hemingway claimed in *The Green Hills of Africa* (1935), for example, that "All modern American literature comes from one book by Mark Twain called *Huck Finn.* ... There was nothing before. There has been nothing as good since."

Author Biography

Best known as Mark Twain, Samuel Clemens was born 30 November 1835 and raised in Hannibal, Missouri. There he absorbed many of the influences that would inform his most lasting contributions to American literature. During his youth, he delighted in the rowdy play of boys on the river and became exposed to the institution of slavery. He began to work as a typesetter for a number of Hannibal newspapers at the age of twelve. In the late 1850s, he became a steamboat pilot on the Mississippi River. This job taught him the dangers of navigating the river at night and gave him a first-hand understanding of the river's beauty and perils. These would later be depicted in the books *Life on the Mississippi* and *The Adventures of Huckleberry Finn.*

After a brief stint as a soldier in the Confederate militia, Clemens went out west, where he worked as a reporter for various newspapers. He contributed both factual reportage and outlandish, burlesque tales. This dual emphasis would characterize his entire career as a journalist. During this phase of his career, in 1863, he adopted the pseudonym Mark Twain, taken from the riverboat slang that means water is at least two fathoms (twelve feet) deep and thus easily travelled.

His second book, *The Innocents Abroad* (1869), a collection of satirical travel letters the author wrote from Europe, was an outstanding success, selling almost seventy thousand copies in its first year. On the heels of this triumph, Clemens married Olivia Langdon and moved to the East, where he lived for the rest of his life. In the East, Clemens had to confront the attitudes of the eastern upper class, a group to which he felt he never belonged. Nevertheless, he did win influential friends, most significantly William Dean Howells, editor of the *Atlantic Monthly.*

Clemens's first two novels, *The Gilded Age* (1873), written with Charles Dudley Warner, and *The Adventures of Tom Sawyer* (1876), a children's book based on his boisterous childhood in Hannibal, won Clemens widespread recognition. Shortly afterwards, he began to compose a sequel to Tom's story, an autobiography of Tom's friend, Huck Finn. He worked sporadically on the book over the next seven years, publishing more travel books and novels in the meantime. When it was finally published, *The Adventures of Huckleberry Finn* was an immediate success, although it was also condemned as inappropriate for children. The book draws on Clemens's childhood in Hannibal, including his memories of the generosity of whites who aided runaway slaves, in addition to the punishments they endured when caught. In fact, in 1841, his father had served on the jury that convicted three whites for aiding the escape of five slaves.

In the 1890s, Clemens's extensive financial speculations caught up with him, and he went bankrupt in the depression of 1893–94. With an eye to paying back his many debts, he wrote a number of works, including continuing adventures of Tom Sawyer and Huck Finn. He spent his final decade dictating his autobiography, which appeared in 1924. Clemens died on 21 April 1910.

Plot Summary

Chapters 1–7: Huck's Escape

Mark Twain begins *The Adventures of Huckleberry Finn* with a notice to the reader. He identifies Huckleberry Finn as "Tom Sawyer's Comrade," and reminds the reader that this novel resumes where *The Adventures of Tom Sawyer* left off: in St. Petersburg, Missouri, on the Mississippi River, "forty to fifty years" before the novel was written (so between 1834 and 1844, before the American Civil War). He tells the reader that several different "dialects are used," which have been written "painstakingly," based on his own "personal familiarity with these several forms of speech."

The novel's title character, Huckleberry Finn, narrates the story. He summarizes the end of *The Adventures of Tom Sawyer,* in which he and Tom discovered a large amount of stolen gold. He lives now with the Widow Douglas, who has taken him in as "her son," and her sister Miss Watson. His father, "Pap," has disappeared:

> Pap hadn't been seen for more than a year, and that was comfortable for me; I didn't want to see him no more. He used to always whale me when he was sober and could get his hands on me; though I used to take to the

woods when he was around.

The widow attempts to "sivilize" Huck, and teach him religion. Huck finds her ways confining. Miss Watson nags him to learn to read, to "set up straight," and to behave. Huck remains superstitious, and he mostly resists the women's influence; after bedtime, he escapes out his window to join Tom Sawyer for new adventures. The boys meet Jim, "Miss Watson's nigger," and they play a trick on him. Jim, like Huck, is superstitious, and when he wakes up he thinks that witches played the trick.

Tom, Huck, and other boys meet in a cave down the river, and form a Gang, a "band of robbers." But Huck tires of the Gang's adventures, because they are only *imaginary*. When Pap shows up in St. Petersburg, he causes Huck some *real* problems. Pap wants Huck's reward money from the end of *The Adventures of Tom Sawyer*. Signs of his son's increased civilization irritate him: the proper clothing, and the ability to read and write. Huck secures his money by "selling" it to Judge Thatcher. Huck's father brings a lawsuit against the judge, but "law" is "a slow business." Eventually Pap kidnaps Huck, and takes him up the river to a shack on the Illinois side of the river. At first, Huck enjoys the return to freedom, but living with his father has its difficulties; "by-and-by pap [gets] too handy with his hick'ry," and he either leaves Huck locked in the cabin alone, or beats him. Huck decides to escape, and cuts a hole in the cabin. After his father lays in some supplies, Huck lays his plans. He catches a canoe as it floats down the river. Left alone, Huck stages his own murder: he kills a wild pig and leaves its blood around the shack and on his jacket, then leaves a fake trail showing a body being dragged to the river. He then loads up the supplies and takes off down river. He stops to camp on Jackson's Island, two miles below St. Petersburg.

Chapters 8–18: Down the River

On the island, Huck feels liberated. Seeing his friends search for his body troubles him only slightly. After a few days, he discovers that he is not alone on the island: Jim has run away from Miss Watson, who had threatened to sell him down the river. Jim's escape troubles Huck, but together they enjoy a good life: fishing, eating, smoking, and sleeping. They find a house floating down the river, with a dead man in it, from which they take some valuables. Huck appreciates the lore that Jim teaches him, but still likes to play tricks. He leaves a dead rattlesnake on Jim's bed, and Jim gets bitten by the snake's mate. He recovers, but interprets the bite as the result of Huck touching a snakeskin—a sure bringer of bad luck. Jim suspects that there is more to come.

One night, Huck dresses as a girl and goes across to town to "get a stirring-up." He discovers that there is a reward offered for Jim and that the island is no longer a safe hiding place. He rushes back to the island, and he and Jim float down the Mississippi, sleeping by day and drifting by night.

Living this way, they get to know each other, and Jim tells Huck about his children. They also have several adventures. They board a wrecked steamboat and steal some ill-gotten goods from three thieves on board, inadvertently leaving them to drown.

Huck and Jim get separated in a fog. They call out, but for hours at a time, they seem lost to each other. Huck falls asleep, and when he awakens, he sees the raft. He sneaks aboard and convinces Jim it was all a dream. When Huck points to evidence of the night's adventure and teases him for being gullible, Jim teaches Huck a lesson:

> "When I got all wore out wid work, en wid de callin' for you, en went to sleep, my heart wuz mos' broke bekase you waz los', en I didn' k'yer no mo' what become er me en de raf'. En when I wake up en fine you back ag'in, all safe en soun', de tears come, en I could 'a' got down on my knees en kiss' yo' foot, I's so thankful. En all you wuz thinkin' 'bout wuz how you could make a fool uv ole Jim wid a lie. Dat truck dab is *trash;* en trash is what people is dat puts dirt on de head er dey fren's en makes 'em ashamed."

… It was fifteen minutes before I could work myself up to go and humble myself to a nigger; but I done it, and I warn't ever sorry for it afterwards, neither. I didn't do him no more mean tricks, and I wouldn't done that one if I'd 'a' knowed it would make him feel that way.

Chapters 19–33: The King and Duke

Huck and Jim plan to drift down to Cairo, Illinois, and then steamboat North, but they realize that they passed Cairo in the fog. A steamboat crashes into their raft and separates them again. Huck swims ashore and is taken in by the Grangerford family, who are embroiled in a feud with another local family, the Shepherdsons. He lives with the Grangerfords, while Jim hides in a nearby swamp and repairs the raft. When the feud erupts into new violence, and Huck's new friend, Buck Grangerford, is killed, Huck and Jim set off once again down the river.

Huck and Jim rescue two "rapscallions," who identify themselves as a duke and a king. They take the prime sleeping quarters on the raft and expect Jim and Huck to wait on them. They employ different schemes to make money along the river. They attend a religious camp-meeting, and the king takes up a collection for himself. In "Arkansaw," they rent a theater and put on a Shakespearean farce called "The Royal Nonesuch." Next, a boy they meet confides that an inheritance awaits one Mr. Wilks, an English gentleman, in his town. Seeing their opportunity, the king and duke assume the identity of Mr. Wilks and his servant, and go to claim the money. Huck feels increasingly uneasy about their unscrupulous behavior, and vows to protect their victims. He hides the cash they try to steal. When the real Mr. Wilks arrives, Huck and Jim try—but fail—to escape without the rascally "king" and "duke."

Next, the king and duke betray Jim as a runaway slave, and "sell" their "rights" to him to a farmer, Silas Phelps. Huck realizes what has happened and determines to rescue Jim. He seeks the Phelps farm. By a stroke of luck, they are relatives of Tom Sawyer's, and mistakenly identify Huck as Tom, come to pay a visit. When Tom arrives a few hours later, he falls in with Huck's deception, pretending to be his brother Sid.

Chapters 34–43: Jim's Rescue

Tom agrees to help Huck rescue Jim. He insists that the escape follow models from all of his favorite prison stories: he smuggles in items past the unwitting Phelpses. He makes Jim sleep with spiders and rats, and write a prison journal on a shirt. He also warns the Phelpses anonymously. In the escape, Tom gets shot in the leg. Jim and Huck each return and are caught in the act of seeking help for Tom.

Finally Tom reveals that Jim is in fact no longer a slave: Miss Watson died and set him free in her will. Tom's Aunt Polly arrives and clears up the case of mistaken identity. Huck, upset by the trick played on him and Jim, accepts Tom's explanation that he wanted "the *adventure"* of the escape. Tom gives Jim forty dollars for his trouble. Now that everyone knows he is still alive, Huck worries about Pap, but Jim tells him not to bother: Pap was the dead man in the house floating down the river. Huck ends the novel with a plan to "light out for the Territory ahead of the rest" before the women try again to "sivilize" him.

Characters

Aunt Polly

Tom Sawyer's guardian. She arrives at the Phelps's farm and reveals Tom and Huck's true identities.

Aunt Sally

See Mrs. Sally Phelps

Boggs

During his travels with the King and Duke in "Arkansaw," Huck meets Boggs, a drunk in Bricksville. Boggs continually curses at townspeople, and despite several warnings, he provokes the wrath of Colonel Sherburn and is killed by him.

Widow Douglas

The Widow Douglas has adopted Huck and attempts to provide a stable home for him. She sends him to school and reads the Bible to him. Although at first Huck finds life with Widow Douglas restrictive, eventually he gets "sort of used to the widow's ways, too, and they warn't so raspy on me." Later, when Huck refers to her, she represents all that is good and decent to him. Nevertheless, at the close of the novel Huck decides to "light out for the Territory" instead of returning to her home.

Media Adaptations

- In the 1930s, *The Adventures of Huckleberry Finn* was adapted twice as a black-and-white film under the title *Huckleberry Finn,* once in 1931 by director Norman Taurog for Paramount, and then in 1939 by MGM. The latter is the most famous of the novel's adaptations. It was directed by Richard Thorpe and starred Mickey Rooney as Huck and Rex Ingram as Jim. The 1939 film is available on video from MGM/UA Home Entertainment.

- An adaptation of the novel was

produced for the "Climax" television program in 1954 by CBS. It starred Thomas Mitchell and John Carradine and is available from Nostalgia Family Video.

- Another film version of the book was released by MGM in 1960, this time in color as *The Adventures of Huckleberry Finn.* Directed by Michael Curtiz, the film starred Eddie Hodges as Huck, Archie Moore as Jim, and Tony Randall as the King. This adaptation is also available on video from MGM/UA Home Entertainment.

- PBS produced a version titled *The Adventures of Huckleberry Finn* for "American Playhouse" in 1986. The movie was directed by Peter H. Hunt and the cast included Sada Thompson, Lillian Gish, Richard Kiley, Jim Dale, and Geraldine Page. It is available from MCA/Universal Home Video.

- Walt Disney produced *The Adventures of Huck Finn* in 1993. This film, starring Elijah Wood as Huck and Courtney B. Vance as Jim, deleted racial epithets and translated the characters' dialects to suit modern tastes. It was directed by Stephen Sommers, who also wrote the screenplay. The film is available from Walt Disney Home Video.

- In 1994, the novel was updated in the film adaptation *Huck and the King of Hearts* produced by Crystal Sky Communications. In this version, Chauncey Leopardi plays Huck, who lives in a trailer park, and Graham Green plays Jim, who is a Native American con artist fleeing a hoodlum from whom he has stolen drug money. The movie was directed by Michael Keusch and written by Chris Sturgeon. It is available on home video.

- The novel has also been recorded on sound cassettes many times since 1980. Unabridged versions are available from Books, Inc. and Books in Motions. Abridged versions are available from Metacom, Listen for Pleasure Ltd., and Time Warner Audiobooks, which released a study guide along with the tape.

The Duke

On their journey down the Mississippi, Huck and Jim pick up two con men who claim to be descendants of royalty. The Duke is a young, poorly dressed man of about thirty. Although they had never met before, the King and Duke soon join forces to concoct a number of scams to play on the innocent inhabitants of the various towns along the riverbanks. Even though he is aware of their true characters, Huck plays along—he has little choice, since the two men are stronger and can turn Jim in at any time. Eventually, however, Huck betrays them when they scheme to cheat the Wilks sisters out of their inheritance. The King and Duke later turn Jim in for a meager reward. The men later get their reward when they are tarred and feathered by an angry crowd. With these two characters, Twain ridicules the aristocratic pretensions of some Americans.

Huck Finn

See Huckleberry Finn

Huckleberry Finn

The narrator and hero of *The Adventures of Huckleberry Finn* is the title character, the fourteen-year-old son of the town drunk who was introduced in *The Adventures of Tom Sawyer*. At the end of that book, Huck was adopted by the Widow Douglas and her sister Miss Watson, who brought him to live in town where he could attend church and school. But at the beginning of *Adventures of Huckleberry Finn,* we learn that their attempts to "sivilize" him have been only partially successful. Huck learns to read and write, but he continues to climb out of his window at night to meet up with Tom Sawyer's gang.

Huck's life in town is abruptly ended when his father returns and kidnaps him, hoping to lay his hands on Huck's fortune. But Huck escapes by faking his own death, and he heads to Jackson's Island. There he meets up with Jim, Miss Watson's slave, who has run away because of her threat to sell him "down the river." The two of them embark on a journey down the Mississippi River and live a life of freedom on the raft, which has become their refuge from society. On their trip, Huck confronts the ethics he has learned from society that tell him Jim is only property and not a human being. By this moral code, his act of helping Jim to escape is a sin. Rather than betray Jim, though, Huck decides, "All right, then, I'll *go* to hell." Huck learns to decide for himself in various situations the right thing to do.

In the last third of the book, Huck defers to Tom Sawyer, whose outlandish schemes to free Jim direct the action. Huck is no longer in charge, and his moral quest appears to have been abandoned. But once Jim is freed, Huck decides he will "light out for the Territory" to escape the civilizing influence of another mother figure, this time Tom's Aunt Sally. For some critics, this decision redeems Huck from the charge that he has allowed Tom to distract him from discovering his inner code of ethics. To others, it means that Twain sees no hope for civilization to redeem itself: because it cannot rid itself of fundamental failures like slavery, someone like Huck must escape its influence altogether.

Pap Finn → antagonist of the novel.

Huck's father, Pap, is an irredeemable drunk who schemes to get Huck's fortune away from him. When he returns to find Huck living at the Widow Douglas's and going to school, he accuses Huck of trying to be better than his father. Pap kidnaps Huck and brings him to a cabin in the woods where he beats his son and confines him to their shack. Pap also submits Huck to his drunken tirades against a free black man, reflecting the attitudes poor southern whites had about blacks who had the right to vote and were highly educated. Shortly after Huck escapes, Pap is killed, although Huck does not learn this until the end of the book.

The Grangerfords

Huck is taken in by the Grangerfords after the raft is broken up by a larger boat on the river. The family is wealthy and Huck is impressed by their gaudily decorated home, although the reader is aware of their shallow faithfulness to ideals of gentility and decorum. Their feud with the Shepherdsons, based on a brutal, senseless code of honor, makes Huck "sick." He leaves after one of the Grangerfords's daughters runs off with one of the Shepherdson boys, and most of the men in the family are killed in the ensuing battle.

Buck Grangerford

The youngest son of the Grangerford family. He is Huck's age, but is killed in the feud with the Shepherdsons. Huck "haint ever heard anything" like how Buck swears after missing an opportunity to kill Harney Shepherdson. Nevertheless, he cries when he discovers Buck's body, "for he was mighty good to me."

Emmeline Grangerford

One of the Grangerfords's daughters, who died in adolescence and left behind a large number of sentimentally morbid poems and drawings that Huck admires. Her family tells Huck, "She warn't particular; she could write about anything ... just so it was sadful."

Jim → shows Hucks compassion + skill.

Jim, a runaway slave who has escaped from his owner, Miss Watson, for fear of being sold to a plantation in New Orleans, is Huck Finn's companion as they travel on a raft down the Mississippi river. He has been recognized by critics as a complex character, at once a superstitious and ignorant minstrel-show stereotype but also an intelligent human being who conveys more depth than the narrator, Huck Finn, is aware of. As their journey progresses, however, Huck does grow to see Jim as more than a stereotype, despite comments like, "he had an uncommon level head for a nigger." Jim confronts Huck's prejudice when he scolds Huck for trying to play a trick on him without taking his feelings into consideration. Pointing to some leaves on the raft, he tells Huck, "dat truck dah is *trash;* en trash is what people is dat puts dirt on de head er dey fren's en makes 'em ashamed." On their journey, Huck becomes aware of Jim's humanity and decides he will assist Jim in his quest to become free.

In the last third of the book, Huck enlists the help of Tom Sawyer to help free Jim, only to learn at the end that Tom knew all along that Jim had been freed by Miss Watson. In this section, critics have argued, Jim is once again cast as a shallow caricature of a gullible slave, and the novel's serious theme of race relations is reduced to a farce. But other critics have seen a consistency of character in Jim throughout the book, as a slave who wears the mask of ignorance and docility as a defense against white oppression, occasionally giving Huck (and the reader) glimpses behind the mask. Forrest G. Robinson has argued that Jim learns Huck "is quite unprepared to tolerate the full unfolding of the human being emergent from behind the mask," and so the real Jim retreats in the last third of the book to ensure that Huck will continue to help him. But according to Chadwick Hansen, Jim is never a "fully-rounded character" in his own right; rather he serves the function of making Huck confront his conscience and overcome society's influence.

The King

On their journey down the Mississippi, Huck and Jim pick up two con men who claim to be descendants of royalty. The King is a bald, grey-bearded man of about seventy years. Although they had never met before, the King and Duke soon join forces to concoct a number of scams to play on the innocent inhabitants of the various towns along the riverbanks. Even though he is aware of their true characters, Huck plays along—he has little choice, since the two men are stronger and can turn Jim in at any time. Eventually, however, Huck betrays them when they scheme to cheat the Wilks sisters out of their inheritance. The King and Duke later turn Jim in for a meager reward. The men later get their reward when they are tarred and feathered by an angry crowd. With these two characters, Twain ridicules the aristocratic pretensions of some Americans.

Mrs. Judith Loftus

A sympathetic woman whom Huck meets while he is dressed up like a girl. She sees through his costume, but inadvertently warns Huck that her husband is on his way to Jackson's Island to capture Jim.

Mrs. Sally Phelps

Tom Sawyer's aunt. When Huck arrives on the Phelps farm, they are expecting Tom, so Huck pretends to be their nephew, while Tom pretends to be his brother, Sid. She good-naturedly scolds "Sid" for pretending to be a stranger and then kissing her unasked.

Reverend Silas Phelps

Tom Sawyer's uncle. When Huck arrives on the Phelps farm, they are expecting Tom, so Huck pretends to be their nephew, while Tom pretends to be his brother, Sid. Phelps appears to be a kindly, good-natured, and trusting man, but he is holding Jim prisoner while waiting for his master to reclaim him.

Tom Sawyer

Tom Sawyer picks up where he left off in *The Adventures of Tom Sawyer* by continuing to lead the other boys in imaginative games based on his reading of romantic adventure literature. But in this novel, his antics are much less innocent and harmless. At the beginning of *Huck Finn,* he provides comic relief in Huck's otherwise straight-laced life at the Widow Douglas's. But his reappearance at the end has troubled many critics. When Tom finds out that Huck is going to free Jim, he wholeheartedly takes up the challenge, creating elaborate schemes to free the man when he could just tell the family that Jim has already been freed by Miss Watson. Neither Huck nor Jim approve of Tom's "adventures," although they feel compelled to submit to his authority in such matters. Many critics have noted the thoughtless, even cruel nature of Tom's games, as they make Jim's life miserable and terrorize Aunt Sally. But Tom is ultimately punished for his forays into fantasy; during Jim's escape he is shot and seriously wounded.

Colonel Sherburn

A Southern aristocrat who kills a drunk, Boggs, in the town of Bricksville, in "Arkansaw." He endures Boggs's taunts and gives him a warning before shooting the man in front of his own daughter. The town threatens to lynch him, but his scornful speech about the cowardice of the average American man and the mobs he participates in breaks up the crowd.

Judge Thatcher

He keeps Huck's money safely out of Pap's hands by "buying" Huck's fortune for a dollar. Later he and the Widow Douglas petition a higher court to take Huck away from his father, but the court's "new judge" says families shouldn't be separated.

Miss Watson

The Widow Douglas's sister and Jim's owner. She represents a view of Christianity that is severe and unforgiving. It is her attempts to "sivilize" Huck that he finds most annoying: "Miss Watson she kept pecking at me, and it got tiresome and lonesome." When Jim overhears her admit the temptation to sell him down South despite her promise not to do so, he runs away. Her guilt at this turn of events leads her to set Jim free in her will.

Wilks sisters

The sisters—Mary Jane, Susan, and Joanna—are orphaned when their guardian uncle, Peter, dies. The King and Duke impersonate their long-lost uncles in an attempt to gain their inheritance. Their trusting and good-hearted nature in the face of the King and Duke's fraud finally drives Huck to take a stand against the two scoundrels.

Themes

Freedom

In *The Adventures of Huckleberry Finn* both Huck and the runaway slave Jim are in flight from a society which labels them as outcasts. Although Huck has been adopted by the Widow Douglas and been accepted into the community of St. Petersburg, he feels hemmed in by the clothes he is made to wear and the models of decorum to which he must adhere. But he also does not belong to the world Pap inhabits. Although he feels more like himself in the backwoods, Pap's drunken rages and attempts to control him force Huck to flee. At the end of the book, after Jim has been freed, Huck decides to continue his own quest for freedom. "I reckon I got to light out for the Territory ahead of the rest, because Aunt Sally she's going to adopt me and sivilize me, and I can't stand it. I been there before." Huck is clearly running from a civilization that attempts to control him, rather than running in pursuit of something tangible. He is representative of the American frontiersman who chooses the unknown over the tyranny of society.

As a slave, Jim has likewise been denied control over his own destiny, and he escapes to prevent being sold down to New Orleans, away from his wife and children. But Jim is chasing a more concrete ideal of freedom than Huck is. For

Jim, freedom means not being a piece of property. Jim explicitly expresses his desire to be free as they approach Cairo and the junction with the Ohio River: "Jim said it made him all over trembly and feverish to be so close to freedom." But after they pass Cairo in the confusion of a foggy night, Jim's quest for freedom is thwarted and he must concentrate on survival. After Jim's capture, Tom and Huck attempt to free him in a farcical series of schemes that actually make escape more difficult and dangerous. Huck indicates that a simple removal of the board that covers the window would allow Jim to escape, but Tom declares that is too easy. "I should *hope* we can find a way that's a little more complicated than *that,* Huck Finn," Tom says. After Jim escapes and is recaptured, Tom reveals that he has been free all along. Miss Watson had died and left him free in her will. The irony of freeing a free man has concerned many critics, who believe Twain might have been commenting on the failure of Reconstruction after the Civil War.

Conscience

Huck's main struggle in the book is with his conscience, the set of morals with which he has been raised. As they begin to approach Cairo, and Jim looks forward to his freedom, Huck says his conscience "got to troubling me so I couldn't rest." He rationalizes that he didn't lure Jim away from his owner, but "conscience up and says every time, 'But you knowed he was running for his freedom, and you could 'a' paddled ashore and told somebody.'"

During this scene he wakes up to the fact that he is helping a slave gain freedom, something he has been brought up to believe is wrong. So in an attempt to relieve his guilt, he sets off for shore, telling Jim he is going to find out if they have passed Cairo, but really intending to turn Jim in. When he meets up with two men looking for a runaway slave, he confronts a true test of conscience, and fails, in his eyes. The two men ask him about the man on board, and Huck protects Jim by making up an elaborate tale about his father who is dying of smallpox, a highly contagious disease. When he returns to the raft, Jim rejoices in his cover-up, but Huck instead is "feeling bad and low, because I knowed very well I had done wrong." He decides that he is naturally bad, and that he only did what made him feel better. Not being able to analyze his actions, Huck fails to recognize that he has taken a stand against a morally corrupt society. Later, after Jim has been turned in by the King and Duke, Huck must again wrestle with his conscience as he decides to play an active role in freeing Jim. Up until this point he had only protected Jim from discovery; now he must help Jim escape, an even more serious crime. But rather than let his "conscience" guide him, Huck listens to his heart, which tells him that Jim is a human being, not property. He turns his back forever on society's ethics and decides he'd rather *"go* to hell" than turn his back on Jim. Through Huck, Twain attacks that part of the conscience that unquestioningly adheres to society's laws and mores, even when they are wrong.

Race and Racism

Probably the most discussed aspect of *Huck Finn* is how it addresses the issue of race. Many critics agree that the book's presentation of the issue is complex or, some say, uneven. No clear-cut stance on race and racism emerges. Despite the fact that Huck comes to respect Jim as a human being, he still reveals his prejudice towards black people. His astonishment at Jim's deep feelings for his family is accompanied by the statement, "I do believe he cared just as much for his people as white folks does for their'n. It don't seem natural, but I reckon it's so." And even after he has decided to help free Jim, Huck indicates that he still does not see black people overall as human beings. When Aunt Sally asks "Tom Sawyer" why he was so late in arriving, he tells her the ship blew a cylinder head. "Good gracious! Anybody hurt?" she asks. "No'm. Killed a nigger." "Well, it's lucky; because sometimes people do get hurt," she responds. As some critics have pointed out, Huck never condemns slavery or racial prejudice in general but seems to find an exception to the rule in Jim. Nevertheless, the fact that Huck does learn to see beyond racial stereotypes in the case of Jim is a profound development, considering his upbringing. He lived in a household with the Widow Douglas and Miss Watson where slaves were owned. And Pap's rantings over a free black man indicate his deep racial prejudice. When confronted with the fact that a free black man was highly educated and could vote, Pap decides he wants nothing to do with a government that has allowed this to happen. He wants the free man, whom he calls "a prowling, thieving, infernal, white-shirted free nigger," to be sold at auction. In other words, all black people are slaves, white man's property, in his eyes. Such are the views on race with which Huck has been raised. But there is no agreement as to what Twain's message on the subject of race is. While some critics view the novel as a satire on racism and a conscious indictment of a racist society, others stress the author's overall ambivalence about race. Critics have had a difficult time reconciling the stereotypical depictions of Jim and other slaves in the book with Huck's desire to free Jim.

Topics for Further Study

- Study the history and form of the minstrel show in the nineteenth century and find evidence in *Adventures of Huckleberry Finn* that

Twain was influenced by minstrels in his creation of the novel.

- Research the history of the novel's censorship in America, and argue for or against the exclusion of *Adventures of Huckleberry Finn* from a school's curriculum.

- Using history texts and primary sources like slave narratives, research the conditions under which slaves lived in the 1840s to gain a deeper understanding of what Jim's life might have been like, and tell Jim's story from his perspective.

Narrator

The Adventures of Huckleberry Finn was a breakthrough in American literature for its presentation of Huck Finn, an adolescent boy who tells the story in his own language. The novel was one of the first in America to employ the child's perspective and employ the vernacular—a language specific to a region or group of people—throughout the book. Many critics have characterized the smoothness of Huck's language as the most unique feature of the book. Lionel Trilling sees Twain's creation of Huck's voice as a measure of his genius. He writes that Huck's language has "the immediacy of the heard voice." Shelley Fisher Fishkin has suggested that Twain created Huck's style of speech from that of a real boy, an African-American child that he met in the early 1870s, combined with dialects of white people he had heard as a child. But Huck's unique perspective is that of a lower-class, southern white child, who has been viewed as an outcast by society. From this position, Huck narrates the story of his encounters with various southern types, sometimes revealing his naivete and, at other times, his acute ability to see through the hypocrisy of his elders. Many readers have commented on Huck's unreliability as a narrator, though, especially in his admiration of the gaudy taste exhibited by the Grangerfords and his inability to see through his own prejudices when he tells Aunt Sally that no one was hurt on board the ship, although a "nigger" was killed.

Setting

Another distinctive aspect of the novel is its setting. Because it takes place when slavery was at its height in America, *The Adventures of Huckleberry Finn* addresses in a roundabout way the prejudices of southern whites that had laid the foundation for slavery and were still omnipresent in the Reconstruction South of Twain's time. The discussion of slavery in the text, then, takes on a new meaning for a post-Civil War audience. It forced them to confront the legacy of slavery in spite of their eagerness to forget its devastating impact and rid themselves of its curse. The physical setting of the novel, most specifically the river and the raft, has also drawn the attention of critics. The

Mississippi River itself serves as a kind of no-man's land in the text, a place outside of society that is governed by different rules. The raft becomes a new world for Huck and Jim, where they can be themselves and make up their own rules by which to live. On either side of the river lies the shore, which represents a return to society. Significantly, it is Huck who makes excursions into towns along the river banks for food, information, and fun. While Huck can be a kind of vagabond, travelling from one place to another without being a part of society, Jim must hide on the raft, the only place where he can be safe.

Burlesque

Burlesques, or parodies of elevated or serious forms of literature, were popular as far back as Shakespeare, but they were also the favorites of working-class theatergoers in America starting in the 1840s. In America, burlesques often poked fun at aristocratic types who were subjected to the lowly conditions of the American city or frontier, and they extolled the virtues of a democracy over the pretensions of Europe's high society. Burlesques also became associated with minstrel shows as they were incorporated into the latter in the 1850s. Mark Twain is well known for his adept adaptations of burlesques in his works. In *The Adventures of Huckleberry Finn* he used the technique to critique the aristocratic pretensions of the King and Duke, and the romantic fantasies of Tom Sawyer. In fact, the last third of the book descends into burlesque, according to the novel's critics, as Tom's outlandish schemes to free Jim take center stage. In addition, some scenes between Jim and Huck are modeled on burlesques, especially their conversation about Frenchmen, in which Jim subtly outsmarts Huck, revealing the wisdom of the supposedly ignorant.

Realism and Regionalism

Mark Twain was a major contributor to the interconnected Realist and Regionalist movements, which flourished from the 1870s to the 1920s. Realism refers to the insistence on authentic details in descriptions of setting and the demand for plausible motivations in character's behaviors. Writers of the Regionalist movement also adhered to these principles as they explored the distinct and diverse regions of post-Civil War America that they feared were being swallowed up by a national culture and economy. Realist and Regionalist techniques are exemplified in *The Adventures of Huckleberry Finn* by the specific and richly detailed setting and the novel's insistence on dialect which attempts to reproduce the natural speech of a variety of characters unique to the Mississippi Valley region. In addition, Huck's momentous decision to free Jim, even if it means going to hell, is seen as a classic episode of Realist fiction because it demonstrates the individual's struggle to make choices based on inner motivations, rather than outside forces.

Historical Context

Slavery

The issue of slavery threatened to divide the nation as early as the Constitutional Convention of 1787, and throughout the years a series of concessions were made on both sides in an effort to keep the union together. One of the most significant of these was the Missouri Compromise of 1820. The furor had begun when Missouri requested to enter the union as a slave state. In order to maintain a balance between free and slave states in the union, Missouri was admitted as a slave state while Maine entered as a free one. And although Congress would not accept Missouri's proposal to ban free blacks from the state, it did allow a provision permitting the state's slaveholders to reclaim runaway slaves from neighboring free states.

Compare & Contrast

- **1840s:** Under the Slave Codes, enacted by individual southern states, slaves could not own property, testify against whites in court, or make contracts. Slave marriages were not recognized by law.

    1884: As the result of Black Codes

enacted by states during Reconstruction, African Americans could now legally marry and own property, but the codes also imposed curfews and segregation. The Fifteenth Amendment granted black men the right to vote, but individual states prohibited them from doing so.

Today: The right to vote is universal for all citizens above the age of eighteen, and other rights are not restricted by race.

- **1840s:** The steamboat was the most popular mode of travel and the Mississippi and Ohio Rivers were the main thoroughfares in the West.

  1884: The railroad had taken over as the means of mass transportation all across America.

  Today: Most goods are transported within the U.S. by truck, and airplanes and cars allow people to travel long distances in short periods of time.

- **1840s:** Means of entertainment were beginning to flourish in America. Among the many new kinds of literature available were slave narratives and romantic adventures. The first minstrel show was staged in 1843.

1884: The field of literature, in the form of books and periodicals, had become the province of the masses. The minstrel show continued to be popular, as did the music of ragtime which was associated with it.

Today: Entertainment, especially film, television, and music, is a multi-billion-dollar industry.

- **1840s:** The Mississippi River ran freely, making travel dangerous, due to snags, large pieces of trees lodged in the river.

    1884: The Mississippi River Commission had been founded in 1879 to improve navigation. Over the next decades, a series of levees were built which also alleviated flooding problems.

    Today: The level of the Mississippi River and its banks are tightly controlled so that navigation is very safe and floods are less frequent.

The federal government's passage of Fugitive Slave Laws was also a compromise to appease southern slaveholders. The first one, passed in 1793, required anyone helping a slave to escape to pay a fine of $500. But by 1850, when a second law was passed, slaveowners had become increasingly insecure about their ability to retain their slaves in the face of abolitionism. The 1850 Fugitive Slave Law increased the fine for abetting a runaway slave to $1000, added the penalty of up to six months in prison, and required that every U.S. citizen assist in the capture of runaways. This law allowed southern slaveowners to claim their fugitive property without requiring them to provide proof of ownership. Whites and blacks in the North were outraged by the law, which effectively implicated all American citizens in the institution of slavery. As a result, many who had previously felt unmoved by the issue became ardent supporters of the abolitionist movement.

Among those who were outraged into action by the Fugitive Slave Law was Harriet Beecher Stowe, whose novel *Uncle Tom's Cabin* (1852) galvanized the North against slavery. Dozens of slave narratives—first hand accounts of the cruelties of slavery—had shown white Northerners a side of slavery that had previously remained hidden, but the impact of Stowe's novel on white Northerners was more widespread. Abraham Lincoln is reported to have said when he met her during the Civil War, "So you're the little lady who started this big war." White southerners also recognized the powerful effect of the national debate on slavery as it was manifested in print, and many southern states, fearing the spread of such agitating ideas to their slaves, passed laws which made it illegal to teach slaves to read. Missouri passed such a law in 1847.

Despite the efforts of southerners to keep slaves in the dark about those who were willing to help them in the North, thousands of slaves did escape to the free states. Many escape routes led to the Ohio River, which formed the southern border of the free states of Illinois and Indiana. The large number of slaves who escaped belied the myths of contented slaves that originated from the South.

Reconstruction

Although *The Adventures of Huckleberry Finn* takes place before the Civil War, it was written in the wake of Reconstruction, the period directly after the Civil War when the confederate states were brought back into the union. The years from 1865 to 1876 witnessed rapid and radical progress in the South, as many schools for blacks were opened, black men gained the right to vote with the passage of the Fifteenth Amendment in 1870, and the Civil Rights Act of 1875 desegregated public places. But these improvements were quickly undermined by new Black Codes in the South that restricted such rights. White southerners felt threatened by Republicans from the North who went south to help direct the course of Reconstruction. Most galling was the new authority of free blacks, many of whom held political office and owned businesses. While prospects did improve somewhat for African Americans during Reconstruction, their perceived authority in the new culture was exaggerated by whites holding on to the theory of white superiority that had justified slavery.

In response to the perceived threat, many terrorist groups were formed to intimidate freed blacks and white Republicans through vigilante violence. The Ku Klux Klan, the most prominent of these new groups, was formed in 1866. Efforts to disband these terrorist groups proved ineffective. By 1876, Democrats had regained control over the South and by 1877, federal troops had withdrawn. Reconstruction and the many rights blacks had gained dissipated as former abolitionists lost interest in the issue of race, and the country became consumed with financial crises and conflicts with Native Americans in the West. Throughout the 1880s and 1890s, new Jim Crow laws segregated public spaces in the South, culminating in the Supreme Court's decision in the case *Plessy v. Ferguson* in 1896, which legalized segregation.

Minstrel Shows

As the first indigenous form of entertainment in America, minstrel shows flourished from the 1830s to the first decade of the twentieth century. In the 1860s, for example, there were more than one hundred minstrel groups in the country. Samuel Clemens recalled his love of minstrel shows in his posthumously published *Autobiography,* writing, "If I could have the nigger show back again in its pristine purity and perfection I should have but little further use for opera." His attraction to black-face entertainment informed *The Adventures of Huckleberry Finn,* where, many critics believe, he used its humorous effects to challenge the racial stereotypes on which it was based.

Minstrel shows featured white men in blackface and outrageous costumes. The men played music, danced, and acted burlesque skits, but the central feature of the shows was the exaggerated imitation of black speech and mannerisms, which produced a stereotype of blacks as docile, happy, and ignorant. The shows also depicted slavery as a natural and benign institution and slaves as contented with their lot. These stereotypes of blacks helped to reinforce attitudes amongst whites that blacks were fundamentally different and inferior. The minstrel show died out as vaudeville, burlesques, and radio became the most popular forms of entertainment.

Critical Overview

When it was first published, responses to *Adventures of Huckleberry Finn* were fairly nonexistent until the Concord Public Library in Massachusetts announced that it was banning the book from its shelves. This action set off a public debate over the merits of the book. The most vocal were those who deemed the book to be unsuitable for children, fearing their corruption by exposure to its lower-class hero. Howard G. Baetzhold reports that beloved children's author Louisa May Alcott said about the book, "if Mr. Clemens cannot think of something better to tell our pure-minded lads and lasses, he had best stop writing books for them." Critics who demanded that literature be uplifting cited rough language, lack of moral values, and a disrespectful stance towards authority as the book's faults. But some critics rallied behind the author and wrote reviews that praised the book as a lasting contribution to American literature.

These early reactions are a fair indication of how the book has been received ever since. On the one hand, respected scholars have claimed the book as the core text of an American literary canon, where it has enjoyed a secure position since the 1950s. As Leo Marx claims, "Everyone agrees that *Huckleberry Finn* is a masterpiece." H. L. Mencken went so far as to dub the novel "perhaps the greatest novel ever written in English." Although some have questioned the formal coherence of the novel, arguing that the ending and Tom's burlesque escapades disrupt the text's quest for freedom, the general consensus has emerged that *The Adventures of Huckleberry Finn* is one of the most important works of American fiction ever written. But despite this resounding stamp of approval from the nation's leading literary scholars, secondary schools around the country have at various times questioned its suitability for students, even going so far as to ban the book. Whereas detractors of the novel from the previous century had been primarily concerned with its lack of decency and moral values, in the wake of the Civil Rights movement, the main concern of administrators, parents, and librarians has become that it promotes racism and demeans African American children with its extensive use of the word "nigger." Ultimately, the fear is that the complexity of the racial issues in the text may be too much for schoolchildren to comprehend. As Peaches Henry explains, "Parents fear that the more obvious aspects of Jim's depiction may over-shadow the more subtle uses to which they are put."

Although in the past there have been sharp contrasts between the responses of scholarly and lay readers of *The Adventures of Huckleberry Finn,* the debate over the book's racial messages has more recently become the center of debate amongst literary scholars as well. The crux of the controversy is whether or not the novel presents an indictment of racism or simply reflects the generally accepted racist attitudes of the time period in which it was written. For most critics, the issue boils down to the depiction of Jim. For some, Jim is nothing more than a minstrel show stereotype, "the archetypal 'good nigger,' who lacks self-respect, dignity, and a sense of self separate from the one whites want him to have," in the words of Julius Lester. In these critics' eyes, Twain reveals his racism when he allows Tom to derail and hence belittle Jim's serious attempts to gain freedom and Huck's efforts to overturn society's view of blacks as property. But to others, a subtle satire on slavery and racism emerges from the text and takes precedence over any stereotypical depictions of African-Americans. Eric Lott argues, for example, "Twain took up the American dilemma (of race) not by avoiding popular racial presentations but by inhabiting them so forcefully that he produced an immanent criticism of them." According to Lott, the use of minstrel show stereotypes, exaggerated and ridiculous depictions of whites's false perceptions of blacks, has the effect of "making nonsense out of America's racial structures." Many critics agree with Lott, seeing the novel itself as a critique of the racism expressed by its narrator, Huck.

For many critics, however, Twain's conscious intentions about racial messages are not the issue. They see instead a variety of perhaps unconscious effects in the novel that point to new ways to understand the text's complex evocation of America's racial predicament. For example, Forrest G. Robinson sees a depth to Jim that he thinks previous scholars have missed. Jim is both the stereotypical "darky" and the complex human being, wearing a mask of contentment and gullibility that represents the kind of prejudice whites have about him as an African American. But behind the mask, the real Jim is a shrewd agent in his own defense. In essence, Robinson argues that whether Twain was aware of it or not, Jim is a complex African American character that reflects the situation of slaves at the time as they attempted to survive in a racist society. Such readings draw attention to the complex ways the novel addresses, in Robinson's words, "the nation's most painful and enduring dilemma." These readings accept Twain's ambivalence and contradictory responses to the issue, rather than attempting to vilify the author or insulate him from accusations of racism. In a related vein of argument, Peaches Henry declares that we may not be able to decide once and for all whether the novel is racist or subversive, but the book deserves our attention because "[t]he insolubility of the race question as regards *Huckleberry Finn* functions as a model of the fundamental racial ambiguity of the American mind-set."

Source

Howard G. Baetzhold, "Samuel Longhorn Clemens," in *Concise Dictionary of American Literary Biography: Realism, Naturalism, and Local Color, 1865–1917,* Gale, 1988, pp. 68–83.

Shelly Fisher Fishkin, *Was Huck Black?: Mark Twain and African-American Voices,* Oxford University Press, 1993.

Chadwick Hansen, "The Character of Jim and the Ending of 'Huckleberry Finn'," in *The Massachusetts Review,* Vol. V, No. 1, Autumn, 1963, pp. 45–66.

Ernest Hemingway, *The Green Hills of Africa,* Scribner, 1935.

Peaches Henry, "The Struggle for Tolerance: Race and Censorship in *Huckleberry Finn,*" in *Satire or Evasion? Black Perspectives on Huckleberry Finn,* edited by James S. Leonard, Thomas A. Tenney, and Thadius Davis, Duke University Press, 1992, pp. 25–48.

Julius Lester, "Morality and *Adventures of Huckleberry Finn,*" in *Satire or Evasion? Black Perspectives on Huckleberry Finn,* edited by James S. Leonard, Thomas A. Tenney, and Thadius Davis, Duke University Press, 1992, pp. 199–207.

Eric Lott, "Mr. Clemens and Jim Crow: Twain, Race, and Blackface," in *Criticism and the Color Line: Desegregating American Literature,* edited by

Henry B. Wonham, Rutgers University Press, 1996, pp. 30–42.

Leo Marx, "Mr. Eliot, Mr. Trilling, and *Huckleberry Finn,*" in *The American Scholar,* Vol. XXII, 1953, pp. 432–40.

H. L. Mencken, "Final Estimate," in his *H. L. Mencken's "Smart Set" Criticism,* edited by William H. Nolte, Cornell University Press, 1968, pp. 182–89.

Forrest G. Robinson, "The Characterization of Jim in *Huckleberry Finn,*" in *Nineteenth-Century Literature,* Vol. XLIII, No. 3, December, 1988, pp. 361–91.

Lionel Trilling, "The Greatness of *Huckleberry Finn,*" in *Huckleberry Finn Among the Critics,* edited by M. Thomas Inge, University Publications of America, 1985, pp. 81–92.

For Further Study

Anthony J. Berret, *Mark Twain and Shakespeare: a Cultural Legacy,* University Press of America, 1993.

> A contextualization of Shakespeare in Twain's time: debates about authorship, Twain's identification with Shakespeare, and popular productions.

Pamela A. Boker, *The Grief Taboo in American Literature: Loss and Prolonged Adolescence in Twain, Melville, and Hemingway,* New York University Press, 1996.

> In this study, Boker looks at the relationship between loss and coming-of-age issues as they are expressed in the works of several prominent American authors.

Richard Bridgman, *Traveling in Mark Twain,* University of California Press, 1987.

> A study of how journeys express several themes in Twain's works.

Bernard DeVoto, *Mark Twain's America* Houghton Mifflin, 1932.

> DeVoto thoroughly analyses the novel's structure and reception.

Shelley Fisher Fishkin, *Lighting Out for the*

Territory: Reflections on Mark Twain and American Culture, Oxford University Press, 1997.

> A new study of how Twain's focus on issues relating to the frontier reflect a uniquely American experience.

Andrew Jay Hoffman, *Twain's Heroes, Twain's Worlds: Mark Twain's Adventures of Huckleberry Finn, A Connecticut Yankee in King Arthur's Court, and Pudd'nhead Wilson,* University of Pennsylvania Press, 1988.

> A study which interprets Twain's characters, including Huck Finn, according to various theories of heroism.

Randall K. Knoper, *Acting Naturally: Mark Twain in the Culture of Performance,* University of California Press, 1995.

> A study which places Twain's work in the popular culture of his time, placing special emphasis on the theatrical forms of entertainment popular in Twain's day and their influence on his work.

Mark Twain: A Collection of Critical Essays, edited by Eric J. Sundquist, Prentice Hall, 1994.

> A collection of scholarly essays, three of which examine *The Adventures of Huckleberry Finn* in particular. A good introduction to

recent scholarly approaches to Twain's work.

Toni Morrison, *Playing in the Dark: Whiteness and the Literary Imagination,* Vintage, 1992, pp. 54–7.

> Morrison interprets the importance of Jim in *The Adventures of Huckleberry Finn* and relates Twain's portrayal to other writers' fascination with and use of African-American characters in American literature.

David R. Sewell, *Mark Twain's Language: Discourse, Dialogue, and Linguistic Variety,* University of California Press, 1987.

> This linguistic study uses sophisticated language theory to analyze Twain's writing. Although a scholarly study, this work is relatively free of jargon.

David Sloane and E. E. Sloane, *Adventures of Huckleberry Finn: American Comic Vision,* Twayne Publishers, 1988.

> This volume in the Twayne "Masterwork Series" examines *Huck Finn* and how fits within the American tradition of comic literature.

J. D. Stahl, *Mark Twain, Culture and Gender: Envisioning America Through Europe,* University of Georgia Press, 1994.

This study looks at two trends in examining Twain's work: first, Twain's treatment of and concern with gender issues; and second, Twain's use of encounters with Europe as a mean to explore and define the American identity.

Lightning Source UK Ltd.
Milton Keynes UK
UKHW021204090320
360022UK00012B/1011